W9-AUQ-315

SandCastle

Sight Words

Snow and More Snow!

Mary Elizabeth Salzmann

Consulting Editor Monica Marx, M.A./Reading Specialist

Published by SandCastle™, an imprint of ABDO Publishing Company, 4940 Viking Drive, Edina, Minnesota 55435.

Printed in the United States.

Credits
Edited by: Pam Price
Curriculum Coordinator: Nancy Tuminelly
Cover and Interior Design and Production: Mighty Media
Photo Credits: Corbis Images, Eyewire Images, PhotoDisc

Library of Congress Cataloging-in-Publication Data

Salzmann, Mary Elizabeth, 1968-
      Snow and more snow! / Mary Elizabeth Salzmann.
          p. cm. -- (Sight words)
      Includes index.
      Summary: Uses simple sentences, photographs, and a brief story to introduce six different words: and, at, be, man, much, were.
      ISBN 1-59197-470-4
      1. Readers (Primary) 2. Vocabulary--Juvenile literature. [1. Reading.] I. Title. II. Series.

PE1119.S234248 2003
428.1--dc21

                                                                                    2003050318

SandCastle™ books are created by a professional team of educators, reading specialists, and content developers around five essential components that include phonemic awareness, phonics, vocabulary, text comprehension, and fluency. All books are written, reviewed, and leveled for guided reading, early intervention reading, and Accelerated Reader® programs and designed for use in shared, guided, and independent reading and writing activities to support a balanced approach to literacy instruction.

Let Us Know

After reading the book, SandCastle would like you to tell us your stories about reading. What is your favorite page? Was there something hard that you needed help with? Share the ups and downs of learning to read. We want to hear from you! To get posted on the ABDO Publishing Company Web site, send us e-mail at:

sandcastle@abdopub.com

SandCastle Level: Beginning

Featured Sight Words

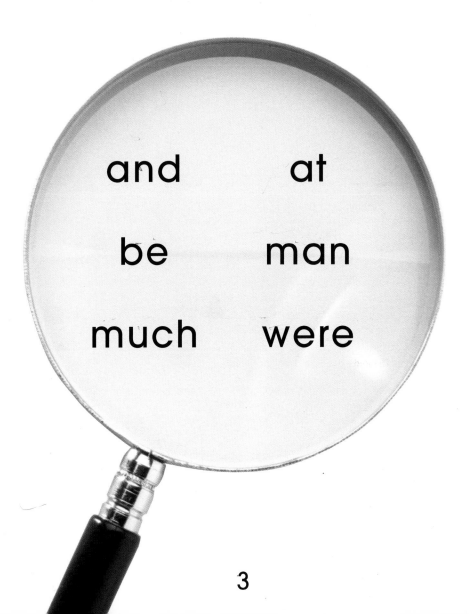

and   at

be   man

much   were

3

Abe has a red hat
and coat.

Wes throws a
snowball at Nina.

Sledding will be fun!

The man is making a snow angel.

I like skiing this much!

Doug and Steve were skiing and snowboarding.

A Snowy Winter Day

Beth and Jan like to be outside in the winter.

Today they made a
man out of snow.

Then they threw
snowballs at Pat.

After that they were
much too tired to
walk home.

Beth and Jan hope
there will be more
snow tomorrow!

More Sight Words in This Book

a	that
day	the
has	their
I	then
in	there
is	they
like	this
of	to
out	will

All words identified as sight words in this book are from Edward Bernard Fry's "First Hundred Instant Sight Words."

Picture Index

coat, p. 5

dad, p. 18

hat, p. 5

red, p. 5

snow, pp. 11, 18, 20

snowball, p. 7

About SandCastle™

A professional team of educators, reading specialists, and content developers created the SandCastle™ series to support young readers as they develop reading skills and strategies and increase their general knowledge. The SandCastle™ series has four levels that correspond to early literacy development in young children. The levels are provided to help teachers and parents select the appropriate books for young readers.

Emerging Readers
(no flags)

Beginning Readers
(1 flag)

Transitional Readers
(2 flags)

Fluent Readers
(3 flags)

These levels are meant only as a guide. All levels are subject to change.

To see a complete list of SandCastle™ books and other nonfiction titles from ABDO Publishing Company, visit www.abdopub.com or contact us at:

4940 Viking Drive, Edina, Minnesota 55435 • 1-800-800-1312 • fax: 1-952-831-1632

ER

Salzmann, Mary
Elizabeth,
1968-

Snow and more snow!

19.93

DATE			

6/24-48x/ 21

BAKER & TAYLOR